SERVANTS, SLAVES, AND SONS

STEVE LONG

Edited by Frank A. DeCenso Jr.

DESTINY IMAGE PUBLISHERS

Scripture is the authors' own. Please note that Destiny Image's publishing style capitalizes certain pronouns in Scripture that refer to the Father, Son, and Holy Spirit, and may differ from some publishers' styles. Take note that the name satan and related names are not capitalized. We choose not to acknowledge him, even to the point of violating grammatical rules.

DESTINY IMAGE® PUBLISHERS, INC.

P.O. Box 310, Shippensburg, PA 17257-0310

"Speaking to the Purposes of God for this Generation
and for the Generations to Come."

This book and all other Destiny Image, Revival Press, Mercy Place, Fresh Bread, Destiny Image Fiction, and Treasure House books are available at Christian bookstores and distributors worldwide.

For a U.S. bookstore nearest you, call 1-800-722-6774.

For more information on international availability, call 717-532-3040.

Reach us on the Internet at www.destinyimage.com.

Digital Edition ISBN: 978-0-7684-1706-7

Trade Paper ISBN: 978-0-7684-1705-0

Originally published in *Catching God's Heart*, ISBN 978-0-7684-3250-3.

Servants, Slaves, and Sons

Steve Long

Servants, Slaves, and Sons

I'm a son. I'm the oldest of six children born to Charles and Mary Long. I was born during my parent's yearlong honeymoon and just before they went back to Malawi, Africa, where they served as missionaries.

My dad and mom met in Malawi while each was on their first term. My father was based in the very south of the nation. Part of his role was to travel to the various villages where there were churches and train the pastors who could not afford to attend Bible school.

My mom was serving in the middle of the nation along with one other gal from her church in London, England. As my mother tells it, my father arrived unannounced one day to visit the local pastor.

He was told that there were two white women in the village. When my parents met, they just knew they were to marry. Not love at first; rather, they just knew that this was the person they were to marry.

So, my father from Toronto and my mother from London spent their honeymoon year in England and Canada. My parents did fall in love and during the year got to know each other's family members and tour a bit of the two nations.

I was born in Toronto, and three months later my parents were back in Malawi, where they started a Bible school, which is still functioning today. Eighteen months later, my brother Richard was born, and another eighteen months later, Jennifer was born.

I'm sure that my parents were very proud to have a son. I know that they loved me—but! The "but" in my life was a lie I believed that hindered my relationships with God, my parents, my siblings, my wife, my two sons, my colleagues, my church, everything.

Want to know what the lie was? Well, you'll have to wait until I tell you the story of two sons who also believed lies.

One of the best known stories in the Bible is from Luke 15 where Jesus tells us about a father and his two sons. The story begins this way:

There was a man who had two sons. The younger one said to his father, "Father, give me my share of the estate." So he divided his property between them (Luke 15:11-12).

Each son was given a portion of the estate. If Jewish custom was followed in the story, the older son would be given a double share. It appears that the older son was given the farm while the younger son was given a large amount of cash.

The story goes on to say that while the money was there, so were the friends. While the money was there, so were the parties and the lifestyle that goes with wild living.

The money is soon gone. So are the friends, and now the country where he lives is in recession. The only job this young Jewish boy can find is to work on a pig farm. The shame and reproach go farther than working with pigs. While he does have a job, his salary is not in money but in food—pigs' food.

One day, as Jesus tells the story, the son comes to his senses and has a revelation. The revelation is this—even the servants, the men and women hired to work on his dad's farm, get better treatment than this!

He makes up his mind that humbling himself and going back to his dad would be better than working with pigs. At his father's farm the servants get a salary, not pig food.

The day comes and he begins the journey home. As he goes he thinks through his past, and without realizing it, a lie from satan slips in and contaminates the truth. The lie so negatively affects the truth that if it were not for the father recognizing the lie and rebuking it, the son would have missed his destiny!

What was the lie? It is one that most of us carry into our relationships, especially our relationship with God. It is so damaging that we can miss the very intimacy with God that He so much wants us to receive!

The Lie: My Past Makes Me Unworthy to Be a Son

This son of a wealthy farmer now believes that the best he can hope for is to be a servant, one of his dad's hired men. Listen as he talks to himself.

I will set out and go back to my father and say to him: Father, I have sinned against Heaven and against you. I am no longer worthy to be called your son; make me like one of your hired men (Luke 15:18-19).

This lie—that his past somehow affects his relationship with his father—is very common. His thinking process goes something like this:

"I sinned against my father by wasting all my inheritance. He won't like that!

"I sinned against God by living a reckless lifestyle. I had sex with women I wasn't married to, I got drunk, and I also broke the law of God and worked with pigs. God won't like that!

"I'm therefore unworthy to be a son. I'm unworthy to be my dad's son and I'm unworthy to be a son of God. My past has caught up to me and I'm now paying the price. My relationship with God and my dad can never be the same again. I'm unworthy!"

Sound familiar? Almost every single person on planet earth has felt this way. Most of us have believed this lie, and because we didn't know it was a lie it has become truth to us!

What is the truth? Well it just so happens that this particular dad represents our Father in Heaven perfectly. That being the case, the father in the story immediately picks up on the lie and challenges it head on.

But the father said to his servants, "Quick! Bring the best robe and put it on him. Put a ring on his finger and sandals on his feet. Bring the fattened calf and kill it. Let's have a feast and celebrate. For this son of mine was dead and is alive again; he was lost and is found." So they began to celebrate (Luke 15:22-24).

The Truth: Sons Are Always Sons—The Occasionally Get Lost

What a father! His first thought is a "but." The Father will hear nothing of the lie and puts into motion a series of acts that brings immediate restoration. The father's orders to the servants overrode the lie of unworthiness. His words beautifully established the boy, who thought he was a servant, as his son! Sons are always sons!

We often face the very same challenge as this young man. Things have happened to us in our past, circumstances came about and stuff happened that we now wish didn't happen. Can we change the past? Rarely. Does our past have to be our future? No! Can we change what we believe about the situation? Absolutely!

This son believed that his relationship with his natural dad would be tainted forever. He also believed that the strict God that he had abandoned wouldn't want him back, either.

Do our negative past experiences affect God and other relationships today? Every time! Especially if we, too, believe the lie that we are unworthy. But if we get the revelation of what our Father in Heaven is really like and accept His truth into our lives, we'll remain as sons.

By the way, ladies, you are a son whether you like it or not! In the Old Testament, women didn't get an inheritance, only the men. The good news is that with a relationship with Jesus, "*There is neither Jew nor Greek, slave nor free, male nor female, for you are all one in Christ Jesus*" (Gal. 3:28).

Guys, if you are thinking you're exempt from a new mind-set, sorry. We have to get our heads around being the "Bride of Christ." God likes taking everyone out of their boxes and putting us in a privileged place!

So the question now needs to be asked—do you see yourself before God as a favored son, or do you see yourself as an unworthy servant? Servants serve. Servants work hard for the master. Servants at best get a fair reward at the end of the day. Servants don't get the intimate relationship that sons do.

In your heart, what do you feel right now? Son or servant? If you responded by saying that you have servant tendencies, I have good news for you. Later, I'm going to lead you through some prayers that will reestablish you as a worthy son! Did you remember that this story had two sons? Let's talk about the older son now. Did you know that he also believed a lie? His lie was just as damaging and it, too, was meant by satan to rob him of his destiny.

As the story continues in Luke 15, the older son is out in the fields and hears the party happening back at the ranch house. He inquires of a servant what is going on and hears about his brother's return. His response is anger.

Imagine the pain of the father on hearing that his older son won't join them on this special day. Just as the father had run to redeem the younger son, the father ran out a second time in one day to find the older brother and bring him home. When the father and older son meet, the son vents angrily. His words betray that he has already believed a lie. Somehow, satan has also influenced this older son.

Did you know that out of your mouth comes what your heart believes? That is good and bad news. The good news is that if we have friends who have ears to hear, they can catch the lies just like this amazing father did.

Did you know that you can also train yourself to catch lies? As we seek after intimacy with the Father, we will slowly begin to hear our own words and recognize that something isn't right. Listen to the older son and see if you can hear his lie.

Look! All these years I've been slaving for you and never disobeyed your orders. Yet you never gave me even a young goat so I could celebrate with my friends. But when this son of yours who has squandered your property with prostitutes comes home, you kill the fattened calf for him! (Luke 15:29-30)

Did you hear it? Did you hear "this son of yours"? He has mentally and emotionally distanced himself from both his brother and father. But that isn't the big one. The big lie is found in his first sentence when he says, "I've been slaving for you." Do you see what he believes? He doesn't see himself as a son but as a slave!

The Lie: I Have to Perform for Love

Look again:

All these years I've been slaving for you and never disobeyed your orders. You never gave me even a young goat so I could celebrate with my friends (Luke 15:29).

Several small lies contribute to the big lie. This older son in his heart believes he has gone from being a son to a slave. He also believes that one qualifies to be a son by obeying orders. Sadly, he also believes that his father was never generous with him nor allowed him to have parties.

A slave is a large step down the scale from a servant. Servants have rights in most cultures—they at least get a salary. Slaves have no rights and get nothing. They are property!

This older son, deep in his heart, believes that nothing he has ever done for his father matters. Mentally, he has positioned himself as a slave—a worthless being, who never will receive any affection or any reward! This lie has also changed his relationship with his father to one of orders and obedience. If he obeys he gets approval, if he disobeys he gets discipline.

Many of us have grown up with this subtle lie embedded in us. Almost all parents reward good behavior and discipline bad behavior. In our formative years, we heard "good girl" and "bad boy" associated with what we did.

The third part of this lie is the statement that his father never even gave him a young goat. Lies are so insidious that they absolutely distort the truth. Do you remember the very first verse of this story? The story began with:

There was a man who had two sons. The younger one said to his father, "*Father, give me my share of the estate.*" *So he divided his property between them* (Luke 15:11-12).

What was the inheritance of the older son? It would appear that a full division of assets took place and the older son was given the farm!

This lie is so mean, so crippling, and so damaging that the older son has lost sight that he now owns the farm! He is still working for his father's approval, even though the father has no more assets to give away! Not only does this son own all the goats, he also owns the farm! Satan has robbed this older son of the farm that his loving father gave him! Listen as the father speaks the truth:

"My son," the father said, "you are always with me, and everything I have is yours" (Luke 15:31).

The Truth: Sons Are Always Sons--They Occasionally Get Confused

The lie that many of us have to deal with is whether God accepts us just for who we are. Do I need to work for His love and approval, just like I had to for my parents to love me? Does God love me more if I'm the first one to church meetings, if I stay the longest, volunteer the most, sacrifice the most, give the most, complain the least?

All these traits are that of an orphan—someone without a father. Sadly, this older son was so confused by the lies his heart believed that he no longer had a dad nor a brother. Confusion reigned in his life! In his own mind he had ceased being a son and now was a slave. He had to do the right things, work the hardest, and try hard to be noticed. Classic orphan-spirit beliefs.

Did you know that most of us view Father God like one of these two sons? The disciples, after three years of being with Jesus, were still servants and slaves. It would appear that none of them knew the Father like Jesus knew the Father. Jesus' promise was that he would "*not leave* [them] *as orphans*" (John 14:18). He wanted each of his men to be a son!

Whole cultures have difficulty seeing God as Father, let alone a loving Father. Did you know that in the Old Testament God is only called "Father" three times? God was not seen as close, cuddly, and on a first-name basis by the nation of Israel. Did you also know that God sent His Son to clarify the issue and bring truth regarding who He is? Jesus called God "Father" about 300 times! Wow, talk about a change of mind-set.

No wonder the disciples had no clue who the Father was! They were speaking a different language than Jesus was regarding the Father. They were thinking like servants and slaves rather than being sons!

Let's go back to my story now. Remember, I'm the firstborn son of missionary parents in Malawi, Africa. I know that my parents love me—but! So, what's the "but"?

The "but" is a lie that came to me from satan when I was about one year old. I've seen this scenario several times as I've had people minister to me. I know it well!

I'm in my bedroom and it's bedtime. The door in my room is a glass paneled one so I can see through into the eating area of our home where my parents were entertaining some of the African leaders.

I don't know why, but I want one of my parents to come and cuddle with me.

I may have needed my diaper changed or was still hungry, I don't know. I can see myself standing up in my crib and calling for my parents.

My parents don't come. I cry out louder. Still no response, so I shake the sides of the crib and yell for my parents. Neither of them seems to notice me, and therefore neither one comes.

I've rationalized this out many times. I can see my parents enjoying their company. They are laughing and either don't hear me or have made the choice not to respond.

For those of you under the age of 45, let me give you some history into child-rearing in the 1950s. The premise was this—kids are to be seen and not heard. Let them cry themselves to sleep, don't give them too much love or attention as it will spoil them.

I've already mentioned that my mom is English. What I didn't tell you was that, while my father was from Toronto, his parents were raised in Scotland. Neither the Scots nor the Brits are known for their extravagant, emotional, expressive love! So I grew up not receiving hugs. I don't remembering hearing the words "I love you," although I'm sure they were spoken. Love seemed to be conditional on my good behavior.

While I was in my crib, waiting for my parents to come, satan visited me. Not in person, but via a thought—a lie. What was whispered in my ear was this: "Your parents don't love you. They've abandoned you emotionally."

As a one-year-old, the circumstances seemed to match the lie. My parents chose not to come to pick me up. They preferred the company of others. They had a nanny that looked after me so that they could devote their full time to the Bible school. I was abandoned!

Did my parents reject me? No! My parents made many large sacrifices for my siblings and me. I know that now, but as a child growing up I felt that I wasn't loved or appreciated. To complicate things, my brother Richard and sister Jennifer were born while we were living in Africa. When I was five my parents took a year off, visiting England and then Canada. As it turned out, my parents felt the call of God to stay in Canada, and my dad became the pastor of a Baptist church.

Three other siblings were born, and now we were a family with six kids. As with most large families, the attention of the parents was divided. It became obvious to me that I wasn't the favorite of either of my parents.

So what do you do to get attention from people you are desperate to have love you? Sports will do it! The only problem was my brother Richard seemed to be more of an athlete than me. He got the attention.

Academics will do it! Well, another problem—both Richard and Jennifer were accelerated. In fact, Richard, though he was 18 months younger than I, caught up to me in school by doing second grade in the mornings and third grade, where I was, in the afternoons. They got the attention.

Good behavior will do it! Well that would be impossible. My sister Jennifer was evil and neither of my parents could see it. (That was my impression at the time—Jennifer is not evil!) They thought everything she did was perfect. She got the attention.

I'll be likeable! Once again, a problem. My youngest siblings, Brian and Liz, were as cute as buttons, and everything they did got them attention.

Ah, but there were other ways to get noticed! I became the clown, and when that didn't work I became rebellious. Even rebel kids get attention. Not for the right reasons, but they do get attention! Still a problem. My middle sister Trish was more rebellious than me! (She's since tamed down and attends our church.)

So how does this relate to my adult years? Fast-forward to when I'm in my thirties. I'm married with two young sons and an amazing wife, Sandra. I'm a Baptist pastor. I'm also still living in the lie that love is earned; love is conditional.

At one of the churches we helped pastor, I was hired specifically to increase the attendance of the church. Finally, a place where I can be loved based on measurable goals! If I can grow the church, I'll be accepted!

The church did grow. I got my financial bonus in half the time the board had expected. But, there is still a love deficit. I know—I'll get my peers to accept and acknowledge me.

Not knowing that I was being driven by lies, our church began to live on the edge. We were the first church in our denomination to have a worship band. We were the first church to let the pastors wear jeans. We were the first church in our network to do "seeker-targeted" church meetings. We had dramas, we had slick marketing, and we got noticed. I was now writing regular articles for our denominational magazine. I was invited to serve on denominational boards.

Without realizing what I was doing, I was using our church family as a tool for my love needs. I didn't intentionally think this up, it just happened; it just became a way of life.

Sandra was trying to reach out to me with unconditional love, but by now I didn't know what that was. I would come home from the church office just after 5 P.M., and within minutes of getting in our house, I would lose my temper with our preschool boys. The house isn't clean enough, the food isn't cooked right, and nothing is good enough! I didn't know it, but I had literally become an older son! I was an orphan and striving for love!

But then! The Bible teaches that, "*We love because he first loved us*" (1 John 4:19). God's unconditional, extravagant, faithful love began to find me!

Perhaps a better way to say it is that I began to let God's unconditional, extravagant, faithful love find me. The "but" for me was a revival that began in Toronto at a church pastored by John and Carol Arnott.

It "just happened" that I met John and Carol in 1992. I was recommended to them by friends as a good conference planner. I helped organize a couple of conferences for their church in 1993 and was even asked to join their church. The timing just wasn't right for us to join Toronto Airport Christian Fellowship (TACF). In January 1994, God visited this church and a worldwide revival began.

Sandra and I were invited by John and Carol to the first extended meeting where Randy Clark, a Vineyard pastor from St. Louis, Missouri, was speaking. We attended and had our very first experience with the Holy Spirit. Wow! What do you say after being on the floor for 20 minutes and experiencing God for the first time? What I felt was peace, but it actually was a huge dose of Father's love for me.

Within ten days of the revival starting, my Baptist church had loaned me to TACF and I found myself helping John and Carol organize the "Toronto Blessing." Within six months, I had joined the pastoral staff. Lots of attention!

I was way behind the rest of the pastors and prayer team in terms of the Spirit, and so at the beginning I just stood on the prayer lines and received. Slowly, I built up enough confidence to pray and minister to others. The primary revelation that God released in this revival was the Father's love. It seemed that everyone was becoming an expert at teaching on the Father's love. Except me.

As the revival moved on, my role was to attend three of the six nightly meetings and bridge the worship team and speaker. I heard over 100 sermons a year for about eight years in a row.

Of the thousand sermons I heard, at least a quarter of them were about the Father's love. Many of them were preached just for me! Specialists such as Jack Winter, Peter and Heather Jackson, Ed and Janet Piorek, Jack and Trish Frost, and James and Denise Jordan regularly spoke on the unconditional, extravagant, faithful love of Father God.

As God's love came my way, I began to see things better. I recognized lies that I had believed. I saw walls that kept love from coming my way and kept me from loving others. The first time I saw the picture of me as a child in the crib was when Will and Madeline Walker ministered to me. They were a part of our pastoral team and knew my parents from Africa days! They were our in-house specialists, and if we were having "emotional" problems we'd go to them. Needless to say, I rarely sought them out for personal ministry. I didn't have problems, others did!

An issue arose in my life, and in the course of needing ministry, Will and Madeline identified rejection and abandonment issues. When they asked Father God to show me the root, this picture came. For the first time in my life I had a memory to go with the pain I was feeling. They led me through a number of repentance prayers for vows, judgments, and soul spirit hurts. I felt a great release of pain as they prayed. That memory would come to me often and I would pray deeper into the various aspects of my lie. That memory of me in the crib was now not a threatening, hurtful place, but one of peace.

Last year I was in that memory again, and the Lord spoke to me of another lie. This one I had not heard before. The Father spoke to me and said something like: "You've been blaming your parents for years for not loving you; that isn't the truth."

What! I asked the Father to clarify this and what He said shocked me so much that I left what I was doing and drove 30 minutes across our city to get verification face to face from my mom. (My dad had died a number of years ago so I couldn't check with him.) What the Father said to me was that the reason why my parents didn't hug me was that I had closed my heart to them, not the other way around! This was a bombshell to me! It was about 8 p.M. when this revelation came.

My mother suffered a stroke a couple years ago and has had to move out of her apartment into a care facility. Her normal bedtime is 9 P.M.', so when I arrived at 8:45 P.M. she was already in bed and about to turn the lights out. I told her about the memory I had as a one year-old and how in my mind over the past years the issue was her and Dad's lack of love to me. I explained to her that the new insight the Father had given me was that I was to blame and not them.

I asked her straight out: "Did I let you hug me and pick me up as a child?"

My mother laughed. Laughing isn't a good sign when you are looking for deep answers to life's hardest questions. She looked at me and said, "*No!* You never liked to be cuddled or picked up; you always wanted to be alone."

Ouch! I now had another set of prayers—repenting and confessing my sins to the Father.

As a pastor I hear both men and women share with me that their relationship with God is distant. They can't seem to engage like they feel others can. I know exactly where they are at. I've lived there. I have the T-shirt; in fact, I made the T-shirts!

For me, intimacy with the Father has been a long journey. I was 50 years of age when that last revelation came to me. I've been a full-time pastor since 1981 and a pastor at TACF since 1994.

Everyone's journey is different. Mine was through the door of dealing with lies. If your journey is similar to mine, I'd like, as promised, to guide you through some ministry now. But first, let me remind you of truth from your Father!

I will be a Father to you, and you will be My sons and daughters, says the Lord Almighty (2 Corinthians 6:18).

The Father's agenda for you is that you will know Him as Father and will know that you are a son or daughter!

But when the time had fully come, God sent His Son, born of a woman, born under law, to redeem those under law, that we might receive the full rights of sons (Galatians 4:4-5).

The Father's desire for you is that you function in the fullness of a son just like Jesus did. In fact, one of the reasons Jesus died was to bring you to the Father! As Paul mentions in Romans 8, there is nothing that can separate me from the Father's love. You are never alone, never!

If you have identified with my story in any way, I'd like you to pray this prayer with me.

Father, would You reveal Yourself to me? Will You help me to see the areas in my past that have incorrectly clouded my view of who You are? I know You are my Father, but I need to know it in my heart, my emotions, and not just in my head.

Ask this question of the Father. After you ask the question, listen and hear what He says to you and write it down. Remember that His sheep hear His voice (see John 10:27). If you are more visual, you may see a picture like my memory as a child in the crib. Here's the question.

Father, what lie has kept me from receiving Your love in that memory?

Ask this question.

Father, what is the truth in that situation?

Ask Jesus to now reveal Himself to you in that situation. The truth is that He is always with us even when we don't see Him. Close your eyes and sense where He is and what He is saying to you or doing for you.

If there are people that you now need to forgive, if there are vows that you've recognized or judgments you know you made, now is a good time to repent, renounce, forgive, and bless.

Father, I forgive (their name) for (what they did or said). I repent of my response of (what did you do?). I bless (their name) today, in Jesus' Name.

One last thing. It would appear from my reading of John 14:16-21 that one of the roles of the Holy Spirit is to bring the Father's love to you and me. Jesus, when talking to His men the night before His death, talked about a special day.

On that day you will realize that I am in My Father, and you are in Me, and I am in you (John 14:20).

I believe that is a direct reference to the experiences they would have in John 20 and Acts 2 when they received the Holy Spirit. Being with Jesus for three years hadn't altered the disciples much in terms of understanding the love of God. But a couple impact sessions with the Holy Spirit sure did!

You and I also need to keep getting full of the Holy Spirit. I'm convinced that He is the agent of Father God to bring His love to you and me. If you close the Holy Spirit off, you close off His love for you!

Normally, I'd get you to close your eyes while I pray this, but since you have to read the prayer, close your eyes as soon as you finish it and linger in His presence.

Holy Spirit, if one of Your roles is to bring the Father's love, please come and visit me now! Holy Spirit, fill me with my Father's love.

Let His love find you today! I know that if you say this prayer every day for a month, you'll become a son! I'm a son!

ABOUT STEVE LONG

Steve Long has been a pastor at the Toronto Airport Christian Fellowship (TACF) and Catch the Fire since 1994. He and his wife, Sandra, have been senior pastors at TACF since 2006, when they took over leadership roles for John and Carol Arnott. The Longs have been active in ministry since the early 1980s, and pastored four congregations (including two church plants) before moving to Mississauga, Ontario to join the Toronto Blessing.

Books by Steve Long

My Healing Belongs to Me

On the Run

The Faith Zone

Servants, Slaves, and Sons

NOTES